WHAT GOOD LITTLE CHURCH GIRLS DON'T ALWAYS LOOK LIKE

Understanding Struggle in Light of the Gospel

What Good Little Church Girls Don't Always Look Like
Understanding Struggle in Light of the Gospel
By Emily R. Oakley

Published by RB Publications
Wichita, Kansas USA

Rebirth Ministries Inc.
1100 E. Grand
Haysville, Kansas 67208
USA

www.rebirthmin.com

ISBN: 978-0-99974695-0
Library of Congress Control Number: 2018961960

Also available in eBook format.
Third Printing.

To my ever-increasing army, thank you.
I am forever grateful for your love, accountability,
and encouragement.

Contents

Foreword

As a leader in the Kansas Assemblies of God Network, I see the value in imparting Biblical truth with love and grace and in practical ways. Diving into this book will offer you just that.

Author Emily Oakley is a dear friend. I'm 30 years her senior but place high value on our friendship. Our relationship consists of lattes and laughter, tears and transparency, wholesome affection and authentic conversation. Often-times our coffee-dates involve deep sharing of biblical insights that produce mutual encouragement and accountability.

These past few years I've had an all access backstage pass to the ups and downs of her life and sense of personal identity. This book will give you helpful snapshots of life-lessons she's unearthed. For me, the standout truth in this book hinges on labels. We find them in shirts, waist bands, and on grocery store shelves. Labels saturate our culture. The purpose of a tag centers on sharing important information. Invisible labels exist and some produce pressure and shame instead of direction and healthy awareness. The invisible label under which Emily lived seems harmless at first glance but you will discover as you vicariously experience her journey that this label shaped but also squelched her true identity. Though her story exposes some sad experiences, she clearly reveals her inner struggle hidden behind the "good little church girl" image.

Emily's experience in working with hurting individuals, her personal experiences, and her therapeutic training have equipped her to speak to many of our world's challenges. Through her ministry, Rebirth Ministries, Emily has the opportunity to present the truths of this book through the mediums of teaching and counseling. Whether you are a parent, a teenage girl, or a mentor to young women, this book will provide support and insights for building a positive, Christ-centered identity.

Do you want to embrace the identity God desires to give you?

Then read on, friend! Enjoy!

Karen Yancey
AGKansas Ministry Network Director
Life-Coach, Conference Speaker and Author

Preface

The purpose of this book is to provide just a snapshot of how God has used my struggles to shape the woman I am today. The pages will be very raw and very vulnerable because I believe relatability is found through the lens of true transparency. This is not meant to be a "yay, Emily," but a "yay, God!" I pray that these pages will offer hope to anyone reading them and awareness that Christians do not have it all figured out just because we go to church on Sunday morning and Bible study throughout the week. We all struggle, but through the cross of Jesus Christ, we all have victory. I hope, more than anything, that you will find victory today in who you are and WHOSE you are.

Through the next nine chapters, I am going to take you on a journey into the process of my own self-discovery. You will not find hard-hitting research (though I will allude to the brilliant work of one my favorite neuroscientists) or a dissertation on the human condition. What you will find is a scriptural understanding of what it means to be a Christian and what that means in light of the human condition. You will find that, through the cross of Christ, all things are possible, and victory is truly attainable. So, as with any good story, let us start at the beginning.

Blessings,
Rev. Emily Oakley

Chapter 1

TEENAGE ANGST

My childhood years were very uneventful. I grew up in a Christian home and went to church every Sunday and Wednesday as if I were a systematically-programmed robot. Relationship with God looked more like ritual and routine as this Christian lifestyle was not something I fully understood. Struggle was obsolete, and if I loved Jesus enough, surely life would be like a magic carpet ride (forgive the umpteen million Disney references this book will have), where all my wildest dreams would come true. I would not ever deal with pain, let alone temptation, because I had been in Bible Quiz and could just quote all that away. While this is most certainly a flawed and incomplete view of not only theology but the Gospel in general, it was the lens through which I looked at life. I had the tendency to breeze right past the part in Scripture where we are told that Christ was tempted in EVERY way as we are tempted, because it did not align with the worldview I had laid out for myself.

Like most teenage girls (or all—let's be real here), I was full of emotion and always on the roller coaster ride of hormones. Some days, life was awesome while others made me, my parents, and my brother insane. But, my flawed scope of who Jesus was and what living for Him really meant hit the wall hard during my sophomore year of high school. My emotional roller coaster plummeted down the next big hill at seventy miles per hour on a crazy collision course. Between poor friend choices, a desire to fix absolutely everything and everyone, no idea who I really was, and circumstances that would impact me well into my adult life, everything I knew about Jesus came to a head. It was not pretty. In fact, it became extremely messy.

You see, I knew that Jesus had died for me and had John 3:16 seemingly memorized since coming into the world. However, I did not have any idea that I could not fix anything in my own strength and had entangled myself in a dangerous web of finding my sole worth and satisfaction in the eyes of people. I entered destructive friendship after destructive friendship and could never fully understand why my life was spiraling out of control. Little did I know, I was the one causing the spiral. I was choosing to embrace an identity that the world was giving me instead of the one I already had. I not only began to hate myself, but I questioned everything everyone had ever told me about God. I asked, "Why are my friendships turning into chaos? Why can I not get a grip on my thought life? God, why are you letting my life spiral out of control?" His loving arms were right there waiting for me; I had just decided to run into the wrong ones. I was the one letting my life continue to spiral completely out of control.

Autonomy develops during the teenage years, and identity really begins to be forged. Poor influences can cause autonomy and identity to move in a destructive manner. This was my experience. Misery became an everyday part of living, and my joy was quickly zapped. I slipped into a deep depression, struggled with cutting, eating disorders, and, after an incident at age fourteen where one of my female friends kissed me at a movie, I struggled with thoughts of same-sex attraction. My identity became wrapped up in struggle, and my angst reached a whole new level. The relationships I had in my life were definitely formidable, but they were not the beneficial kind. For the next ten years, my life would be riddled with unbridled shame that I could not really speak about, because I was a good little church girl, and I was not supposed to struggle. I had convinced myself of that lie for several years. It was a lie that led me to walk down a destructive path. Thankfully, I no longer remember what it feels like to live that low, but God still uses those years in my life as a reminder of His grace and mercy even when I had no clue good could come from pain. I am still not entirely sure why I convinced myself that I was not supposed to struggle, and that struggling with feelings of same-sex attraction made me exempt from anything good that God wanted to do in my life. Thankfully, Jesus has healed me of this misconception and continues to teach me to have grace for myself in the moments when I have shortcomings and weakness.

> Clearly, struggle is all over the Scriptures, but church culture seems to have created a cone of silence.

Clearly, struggle is all over the Scriptures, but church culture seems to have created a cone of silence. Hot topics and everyday issues are not often widely discussed in church settings (they are being addressed more lately because their increasing prevalence is practically forcing them to be dealt with), but the pressures that individuals (not just teenagers) face is mounting. In my work at Teen Challenge, a Christ-centered rehabilitation program, I encountered several girls who had no idea that Jesus could still love them because of everything they struggled with and went through. The concept that no matter what sin they had in their lives, Jesus still loves them, was a lost one. This deception kept them from wanting to fully e brace the life Jesus intended for them. It was not until they surrendered the identity they had made for themselves, and embraced the one Jesus had already died to give them, that true freedom really began to take shape and root in their hearts and lives. As Christians, it is critical that we give voice to these pressing cultural issues and that this voice is communicating love with truth.

So why are Christians not talking? Why are Christians letting a secular worldview speak louder than the Word of God? What in our lens needs to shift to openly discuss the hurt and pain so many are wrapped up in? Better yet, how do we bring truth to the darkness? **Shame should not be the** Shame should not be the dictator **dictator of our lives. Its** of our lives. Its place is far away, nev- **place is far away, never** er again to be touched. This means **again to be touched.** we lay shame at the feet of Jesus and do not pick it back up. This means we understand that conviction is not the same as condemnation.

So many like me believed (or still do believe) that something must be completely wrong because their lives are full of struggle. They almost feel like Christians should be impermeable to the garbage this world throws at them. Unfortunately, though we love Jesus, we are still fallible humans. Struggle does not mean we have failed as Christians. Everyone struggles with something, no matter

8

what that something may be. However, God has gifted each of us with the power of choice and the ability to overcome. This gift does not mean that our struggles will always magically vanish (though God is very capable of removing them), but it means that we shift our lens from looking at the circumstance to looking to the very Creator of life. We shift our attitudes from "I can't" to "Through Christ, I will and most certainly can." Life, though sometimes difficult, does not have to be full of angst. Through the blood of Jesus Christ, we are victorious.

As I look at teenagers now, I see the things that consume their lives and wish they would believe me if I told them that, ten years from now, some of the things they are dealing with are not really going to matter. The drama with the girl in English class or the fact that parents are too old to remember how it feels to be fifteen will not matter in only a matter of years (or sometimes weeks or months). In the moment, though, it seems like their whole world will never be whole again. What I have learned is that pain is real to the person experiencing it, no matter how ludicrous it may seem.

I remember one of the teenage girls I mentored and the tumultuous effects she experienced after her boyfriend of five minutes (just kidding, it was at least five days) broke up with her. Now, I am sure most of us can relate, or maybe we were that girl who had her heart broken after five magical days of bliss and happiness. (I'll be honest here; I was one of those girls). I am sure we can also relate to the other side of that where we remind these girls that their life has far more significance than one boy in a very short-term relationship. However, in the middle of dealing with teenage (or even adult) angst, everyone wants to know that people care, and that people hear our needs. What do people crave most? We need authenticity and a place to just be real. On top of that, people crave true and unbridled love. That is why Disney is so popular. It always presents fairytale, though unrealistic, love.

So, we can either sit with people in their pain and provide empathy, love and support, or we can automatically dismiss them. Now, I am not saying we must coddle or treat the death of a blip of a relationship like the start of World War III. Clearly, part of the responsibility of being a Christ-follower is also being loving enough to tell people the hard stuff. However, we can always approach hard truths with love and grace. I have been told multiple times that it is not what we say but how we say it that can truly make all the difference in the world to someone who is really in pain.

The adults who had to deal with me when I was a teenager had quite the task. I was full of emotion and full of energy, and these two together can be quite the lethal combination. However, these adults loved me where I was and took time to hear the things that hurt me. They did not dismiss me as some ridiculous little child, but they always made me feel like I mattered and so did my hurt. Did they sometimes have to tell me that I needed to let it go and move forward because it was not worth the time? Yes, but again, this was all done through the lens of empathy, love, and grace. When we take five seconds to remember how Jesus loves us in our angst, it is much easier to love others in the midst of theirs.

Every time I was frustrated with my girls at Teen Challenge, God was kind enough to remind me that I created plenty of difficult moments myself and that these girls were broken and in need of God's love. Now, my issues and these girls' issues are not the same, but they are still issues. God continues to teach me to handle situations with truth but to also handle them with love. The most constructive place to experience "criticism" is in the arms of some-one you know really cares about you. Does this make it comfortable? No, but it does make it understood that they only have your best interests at heart.

The most constructive place to experience "criticism" is in the arms of someone you know really cares about you.

There is a very popular ex-pression that people like to toss around, and that is "The struggle is real." There is so much truth to that old statement. We all struggle, we all have hurts, and we all go through hard seasons. However, we each get the unique and wonderful opportunity to choose how we frame these struggles, and how we let them shape us for the rest of our lives. Perspective is everything, and thankfully our Christian perspective is inclined toward hope, even though we can recognize that "the struggle is real."

If you are reading this today and are struggling and feeling discouraged, know that you are not alone. I hope we can all blow the misconception out of the water that just because we are Christians means that we do not struggle and face hardship. I also hope that we can learn how to better walk with other people as they face hurt and difficulty. We all desire grace, but sometimes it is much harder to lend that grace to other people, especial-ly when we feel like they should know better. So, as we journey together, let's take a moment

If you are reading this today and are struggling and feeling discouraged, know that you are not alone.

to view struggle through a different lens, a godly lens. Maybe, just maybe, we can shift a paradigm in a culture inundated with false truths and built on shaky foundations. Let us begin to unpack what good little church girls actually look like.

Discussion Questions

1. What does struggle mean in your life?

_____

_____

_____

_____

2. How have you allowed struggle to shape your perspective?

_____

_____

_____

_____

3. How do you want other people to approach you when you struggle?

_____

_____

_____

_____

4. How do you want to approach others in their struggle?

_____

_____

_____

_____

Chapter 2
RIDDLED WITH SHAME

Shame is a tricky business, and if you have the chance to read it, Christine Caine's book, *Unashamed*, is a great resource for understanding this difficult topic and better ways to tackle it. Shame plagues too many minds and keeps too many people living in a defeated lifestyle. Shame creeps in at the most inopportune times and tells us that we will never be able to live the victorious life that God intended. It hides in the shadows and wants us to feel the looming cloud it brings no matter where it goes. The words it declares are those of never amounting to anything and that who we are, not what we have done, is wrong.

I am all too familiar with shame. The battle in my mind became very real the moment I started struggling with thoughts of homosexuality. I knew that was not the life God intended, and I also explicitly knew what Scripture said about it. So why was I struggling with it? What had I done wrong? Why did one moment in my life have such a dramatic impact? I would not have those answers for several years, but I spent most of my time convinced that I would never be able to be successful in ministry. I knew I had been called, but wondered if God would really be able to use someone as disgusting and shameful as me? I thought that if the people in my life really knew what I struggled with and what plagued my mind, they would not want anything to do with me. While I know this to be far from the truth now, I walked through most of my teenaged and early adult years carrying a crushing weight of never feeling like I would have the capacity to overcome my thoughts. There was no way that Jesus could love me because I could not even love myself.

That is exactly what the enemy wants you to believe— that you are unlovable. This is so unbelievably far from the truth, yet shame makes us believe that no one will ever be able to love who or what we are. Shame also wants you to maintain silence. It is amazing how many misconceptions and lies can get blown up in our heads when we allow them to fester and stew in darkness without sharing. If you are anything like me, shame can also make you constantly fearful of rejection. Yet another lie of shame.

Believing that we have no value will make shame a giant it should never be. The Book of Romans says that we all mess up, but the beauty of the Gospel is that we have freedom in Christ.[1] No matter what you have done, no matter what you might be struggling with today, Jesus loves you and desires a real relationship with you. Nothing and no one can ever take

Believing that we have no value will make shame a giant it should never be.

---

[1] Romans 3:23

that desire in our Heavenly Father's heart away. It is oh so important to not let the enemy's commentary be the commentary we listen to. If we do, we will forever be hindered and unable to move past our shortcomings. Jesus never intends for us to live hindered, unable to move forward in the freedom we truly have. Let the truth of who Jesus says you are outweigh the enemy's claim that you do not have value.

I remember the moment that Jesus told me I needed to share what I was dealing with. It was Christmas break of my freshman year of college, and I was home having a sleepover with a friend. Of course, in the wee hours of the morning, the Holy Spirit decided to prompt me to open a ginormous (like the movie Elf) can of worms. I tried my absolute best to ignore the tugging (and, honestly, what at the time felt like nagging) at my heart because I just did not want to deal with it. After what felt like hours, even though it was probably only minutes, I decided to trust the loving prompting of my heavenly Father and open up. So, I did. In the pitch black where nobody could see me or every single tear streaming down my face.

To this day, my friend Alina's reaction will stay with me because it was honestly the most biblical representation of love I could have felt at that moment. She gently wrapped her arms around me and spoke the words I was petrified I would never hear: "I still love you." Cue the water works even further. She did not run away. She did not yell at me that I was some terrible human being. She did exactly what Jesus did—loved me right where I was. Not only that, but the next thing she said would stay with me forever: "Emily, I know who you are. That's not it." That very statement sent me on a path to self-discovery and understanding that my identity was in the One who created me, not in the mangled mess that tried to daily ensnare my mind. Alina loved me where I was, but she did not let me stay there. You see, the world wants to tell us that if you truly love someone, you will let them be what they feel. I hate to break it to you, but that's not love; that is deception. The Word of God is explicitly clear on sin and its place in our lives, but it is also clear that we will all struggle. In that moment, my friend Alina understood that I was struggling. She knew it did not have to be the defining moment of my life, nor did it have to be something that bogged me down for the rest of my life. It was my struggle, sure, but it was not (and is not) who I am.

Shame wanted to keep me silent. Shame wanted me to sit on my secret and feel like a disgusting waste of space for the rest of my life. But, God. God never intended for me to struggle alone or in fear. He wanted to let the truth of His love invade every ounce of the broken spaces of my life. For the first time in four years, I felt like I could be free. I felt like I did not have to hide under the covers of my shame-laced blanket. For the first time, I could begin to throw off the weights that had held me bound for years. Though it would take several years and several more tear-stained moments, that moment of encouragement began the journey that would forever alter my view on shame.

I was not some horrible Christian because I had a struggle; I was a human one. I could still do ministry, and even yet, I could do it effectively because ministry is not about me. It is about the truth, power, and love of Jesus Christ. Little did I know our culture would live driven by feelings or have so many questions surrounding the gay community, but I know my story is for such a time as this. Too

16

many individuals feel like their past keeps them from ever having a real impact on the world. What we often forget is that God works EVERYTHING, if we allow it, for our good and His ultimate glory.[2] We are all human, and every rock star of the faith has experienced difficulty. Even in the midst of hardship, we see that living victoriously is possible through the power of the Holy Spirit.

One of my favorite "rock stars" is King David. David is a man whom Scripture describes as being after God's own heart. However, most of us know how that story goes. Allow me to share the Reader's Digest version. 2 Samuel presents David as a man who clearly has an anointing of the Lord but, a man who also has a whole lot of fleshly desires. David gazes out and sees a beautiful woman bathing on a roof. (Anyone else think that would be a bit chilly?) David does not make himself look away, but he decides he wants to have her. He then commits adultery with a woman who is already married, gets this girl pregnant, and then kills off her husband who is a loyal solider in his army. (For further detail on this incredible story, please visit 2 Samuel!)

King David knows what he did is wrong, but he thinks he has gotten away with it until the prophet Nathan calls him on the carpet and tells David what the consequences of his actions will be. Now David has a few choices: let this be the altering moment that crushes him or the moment that catapults him forward into a life even more committed to God. Thankfully, King David chose the latter. He could have lived his life riddled by shame and never allowed himself to move forward from his bad choices. David experienced consequences for his actions, much like all of us do. However, he

---

[2] Romans 8:28; 2 Samuel 11

17

moved forward and became one of the greatest kings to be recorded in all of history. Like David, we get to decide our narrative, and we get to decide how many pages shame gets to pen.

Shame wants you to keep your eyes focused on your struggle. It wants you to feel disgusting and miserable. The current season of life that I am in has been full of transition, and though not full of shame, it's been full of distraction. It is easy to keep my eyes everywhere but on Jesus. Through the entirety of this season, I have felt the heavenly Father so kindly whisper to me three very profound words: "Eyes on Me." When we keep our eyes on the blood and redemptive work of Christ, shame holds no power. Though it wants to keep our attention, it does not have to. Shame only has the power insofar as we let it have power. Shame can also keep us from fulfilling our purpose. Each of us was put on this planet to show God's glory in one way or another, and if we listen to a narrative God did not intend for us to grab hold of, it will hinder our ability to move forward in the calling God has placed on our lives. Shame keeps us from moving forward.

Understanding shame does not mean feelings are not real, because, believe me, I know they are. My **We get to choose the paths our minds take and if we want to accept God's truth.** hope is that if you are reading this today, and you feel worthless and disgusting, you will know you are valued and loved. You will know that no matter your past, if you allow Him to, God's got your present and your future. And when the world wants you to look around, look up. I promise you, eyes of love and care will look back. They will challenge you to live in a way you have never lived before, and that is a beautiful thing. Shame does not hold the power over us. We have the ability to remember that we are not crippled by the decisions of the past.

We get to choose the paths our minds take and if we want to accept God's truth. Shame does not have to be the guiding force in our lives. We do not have to spend our whole lives looking at temporary circumstances that might be gone in days, months, or even years. The one thing that will constantly remain the same is Christ and His love.

Sometimes, people allow themselves to become agents of shame. We live in a world that likes to be really cruel at times. People say and do hurtful things because they are in a place where they are feeling hurt. In the next chapter, we will dive even further into what it means to have an identity and where it should be anchored, but for now, let me just encourage you that a lot of those people's voices will not be around forever. Sometimes, it might be a family member or a negative friend, but no matter what toxins they are spewing, we get to choose what we accept as truth.

When we are inundated with hurtful actions or lies, it can be really easy to fall into the trap that shame likes to lay out for us. It is so much easier to just give into the negative thoughts because fighting requires a lot of gumption that we sometimes just do not have. But, the moment we believe God's truth about who we are, shame loses its power. You get to choose which road to take, but the road to shame will always lead to much greater and much deeper heartache.

I have learned that people **Sin tears at the fabric of** crave authenticity and transparen- **all our lives, which is why** cy from those in ministry. The more real **grace is such a rich** you are, the less lonely you make other people feel. **tapestry.** Knowing that we are all working through this life together keeps isolation at bay. Our struggles might not all be the same, but our hu-

19

manity is. Sin tears at the fabric of all our lives, which is why grace is such a rich tapestry. Sharing with one another (obviously in a safe space and not to the entire world) gives a true place of healing. Vulnerability allows such a unique space, and it is a space that sharing my story can provide. Vulnerability also helps keep shame in its rightful place.

Every time I have allowed myself to be vulnerable, it has loosened shame's grip more and more. Does this mean I always share my past struggles without a few nerves? No, but it means that I have finally figured out that shame has not written my story; the cross of Jesus Christ has. There is not a specified time or place to be vulnerable, but we are meant to have an inner-circle for a reason. Sometimes, vulnerability might be in the office of a professional who can offer an objective outlook on the road we are walking. I know the life-changing impact a good, biblical counseling experience can have. God intends for us to walk through life with other people in tandem. Through such mediums as counseling and a great circle, we really can experience true freedom.

We get to choose whether we listen to shame or the Holy Spirit. Once we discover that shame has no power over us, it is time to figure out who we are. Let's dive into what a true and God-given identity looks like.

Discussion Questions

1. How do you define shame?

_____

_____

_____

_____

2. Are there any areas of your life where you are letting shame speak louder than the Holy Spirit?

_____

_____

_____

_____

3. How can you keep shame from ruling your life?

_____

_____

_____

_____

Chapter 3
DISCOVERING IDENTITY

Who am I? This is a timeless question that we ask ourselves at multiple points in our lives. What makes us tick; what defines us? If we take a look at the world around us, we get a pretty scattered picture of just exactly who we are. The world wants us to be defined by sexual orientation, success, our careers, how much other people like us, how many friends we have, whether we have a significant other, our children, or how many likes we can get on social media. There is also a strong push to live based upon how we feel. Those of us who have spent any time around people understand that there is a whole lot of emotional whiplash that comes with living based on feelings. Feelings are not anything to base our lives on. It is okay to have them, but feelings should not be our defining factor. Our world is inundated with temporary measures of what should be an eternal identity. Who we are is wrapped up in one place: the cross of Jesus

Christ.

If you are like any other human ever, you have had a misplaced identity. We all have. While the list I mentioned of ways the world wants us to identify ourselves is not exhaustive, hopefully it has hit the high points. Placing identity in any place other than Jesus Christ leads to an unstable foundation. It invites a life-long battle with shame and doubt. Anything other than a foundation built on Jesus cracks under pressure and will inevitably lead to disappointment. We are watching our world go through the craziest identity crisis, and it is not getting any better. Basing identity on feelings or circumstance like culture suggests, is a very temporal identity. When the fire has been put out and the smoke begins to clear, we are left with a broken and fragmented reality that was never meant to be our definition. The only way to avoid such a reality is to have a strong foundation.

Personality tests are some of my favorite things in the whole wide world because I love learning about other people and how we all tick as human beings. I also really enjoy personality tests because they have nothing to do with math and are not related to tasks. So, based on Myers Briggs, I am an ENFP, which basically means that I am a very charismatic person who feels very deeply and desires a deep, emotional connection with the people in my life. Part of this means that I have all the emotions. As a very emotion-prone human being, I have spent way too much of my life being identified by how I feel or what I struggle with. Personality tests, however, do not paint a complete picture of who we are because each of us is an unique individual. Though I never identified as gay, I had an understanding of the mindset and felt like I would never be able to be anyone but someone who struggled with homosexuality.

In the middle of my struggle, I had no concept of an identity in Jesus, and I spent too much time on an emotional roller coaster ride. We all struggle, even though **Feelings change, and we** everyone's struggle does not look **do ourselves a disservice** the same. However, we do not **when we treat life as if it** have to buy into the misconcep- **is based just on how we** tion that our feelings are something to base our whole lives' **feel.** worth on. Feelingschange, and we do ourselves a disservice when we treat life as if it is based just on how we feel.

Many of us also find our identity in the relationships around us, or in the tasks we accomplish. For me, it has always been difficult to not identity myself by the people around me or what they thought of me. If a relationship crumbled, my world crumbled. This, in turn, caused serious trust issues and an inability to see that the Master Orchestrator was bringing everything together for my good. Codependency, which is an unhealthy emotional attachment where you put all your emotional eggs in another person's basket, became a big problem for me. I wanted to be able to be everyone's everything, a role only God is intended to fill. I also took on the responsibility of trying to meet others' every emotional need which left me tapped out and completely exhausted. I had to learn boundaries in order to rediscover who I was outside of the scope of any one person. People in our lives are not a bad thing; in fact, we are meant to be in community. However, people being our everything creates chasms that are often hard to see coming.

Many also find their identities in their success or careers. Life can become a series of checklists or how quickly one can climb the corporate ladder. While we should always cherish and take care of our relationships and steward and work hard with our tasks, we can be neither consumed nor defined by our relationships and tasks. Climbing the ladder will only take people so far and will not be the thing that keeps everyone happy. So many successful people struggle with depression or even suicide because they are trying to base who they are on the title behind their name or the corner office that they worked thirty-five years to achieve. As I said before, success is not a bad thing; but it can become a negative influence when it becomes more important than our relationship with the King of Kings. Keeping our eyes focused on the external circumstance hin-ders our ability to look up to see the true Author of peace. Every part of our lives should be ordered in light of who Jesus is and the truth of the Gospel.

Thankfully, God brought (and continues to bring) people into my life who reminded me that my identity is found in no place other than Jesus Christ. They never once shamed me or made me feel like a disgusting person because I struggled. Instead, they wrapped their arms around me and helped me on a new adventure of discover-ing who and whose I am. I still have people who lovingly remind me of who I am and that it is not based on what I can do for other people. We are all on a journey and understand-ing who we are is critical to being all

It takes time to remove the broken foundation that has shaped one's core. Though it is shaky and full of cracks, it is often deeply rooted.

God wants us to be. We can all have access to these God-given reminders of who we are if we allow the Holy Spirit to convict us and move on our hearts.

It takes time to remove the broken foundation that has shaped one's core. Though it is shaky and full of cracks, it is often deeply rooted. If it is not replaced with the solid foundation of who the

Word says we are, the broken foundation will remain. I lived life tossed by the waves of emotion for far too long and made myself much more tired and overwhelmed than I ever needed to be. The people in our lives (though not all) will change, the seasons will change, our careers may change, or even our addresses may change. The only security we have is being children of the King. Let that truth anchor you for the rest of your days. As you walk through the process of exchanging a shaky foundation for a solid one, have grace for yourself. This is a difficult process and sometimes arduous. As Dr. Caroline Leaf talks about in her book *"Switch on Your Brain,"* we are having to re-wire a complete new way of thinking when we exchange our old foundation.[3] Thankfully, we do not walk through this journey alone, and, as we put forth the effort to truly experience the change, God will bring about the healing.

With a shaky and misplaced identity comes a misplaced focus. Satan wants us to spend so much time focusing on our struggles or our sins that we forget to put our eyes on the only one who can pull us out of our muck and mire. As I mentioned earlier, I have heard one over-arching theme coming from God: "Eyes on me." Of course, this seems like a completely basic concept, but it is hard to do this when we are bombarded with everything else. Until we get our eyes on Jesus, we can never really understand who we are supposed to be. We can never understand that who we are is defined by the most beautiful redemption story and anchors itself in the cross of Calvary. I want to quit walking around in life saying, "Hi, my name is Emily. I struggle, I am also a counselor and a pastor, and I run around like a chicken with my head cut off sometimes because I do not know how

---

[3] Leaf, Caroline. *Switch On Your Brain: The Key To Peak Happiness and Health.* Grand Rapids, Mich.: Baker Books, 2013.

to sit still." What I should say is, "Hi, my name is Emily, and I am a daughter of the King." We spend way too much of our lives focused on temporal meaning when we were meant for an eternal purpose.

I am not saying it is bad to be excited when we accomplish goals, or get married, or become a parent, or whatever else you can insert here. Please, do a happy dance! But think of the athlete who wraps up their whole life in a sport and then has it ripped away because of an injury. For many, the sport is their whole life, and when it is gone, it is hard to know who they are. For the business person, a collapsing company creates a void that seems overwhelming and hard to escape. Please do not read this to mean that everyone is be expected to be Superman or that Jesus expects this either. Pain happens, and hurt is very real, but we get to shape our perspective on the events or the hurts that we face. The beauty of being a Christ-follower is that our identity is forever sealed and does not have to be marred by heartache and pain. As the Apostle Paul tells us in his writings, God has placed His seal of ownership on us.[4] We are His. Though difficulties will shape our character and oftentimes lead us on a path we would have never anticipated, they are not the core of who we are. My life has had lots of change, and it is a comfort to know that my identity never will change.

The Bible also tells us that we have been adopted into God's royal family and have been made coheirs with Christ. Through the blood of Jesus, we now get to be a part of the coolest family ever created. We were chosen, not because of anything we did, but because God loved us enough to say we were worth the sacrifice. I know my own life, and I know that nothing I have done or ever will

---

[4] 2 Corinthians 1:22

28

do makes me worthy of that sacrifice. I am incredibly grateful for the gift. Grace provides the most incredible lens for us to view life. I actually have the coolest snapshot of adoption, and I am grateful because it has made me that much more appreciative of the fact that God chose me. My superhero, comic-book loving, kind-hearted, and goofball of a father also chose me. When I was almost two, my parents got married, and my dad decided that he wanted me to carry his last name. My biological father has never been a part of the picture, but when my parents got married, my dad chose to be my father. I have always had so much respect for my mom because she would have much rather raised me by herself than put me in a bad living situation, so that is what she did for the first year of my life. However, in a beautiful moment at the Sedgwick County Courthouse in Wichita, Kansas, my dad signed a piece of paper that made me an Oakley. The picture we have of us right after is one of my favorites because you see the gleeful look of a new father and the complete comfort of a little girl in the arms of the man who would forever be her Superman.

My dad picked me. He did not have to, but he chose to. He gave me his last name; he gave me a place to belong; he gave me a home. Not only that, but he gave me a family. Jesus did that and so much more when He took our place on Calvary. He did not have to choose us or sacrifice His life, but He did so willingly. I know my dad did not choose me with the understanding that I would be the perfect kid. (I mean, I did not do anything completely ridiculous, but I was still a teenager and a rebellious child at points!) In the same regard, God knows we will not be perfect. He knew when He chose us that we would make a mess of things. But, He gives us tools and equips us to move forward and make healthy decisions. Does this mean we do not have moments where we slip up? Of course not, but it does mean that we actively pursue the life He intended for us, forsaking the life we leave behind when we become new creations.[5]

John 15:1-11 gives us a great illustration of being a part of the vine. We are all branches connected to the eternal source that is Jesus Christ. As we continue to walk out this Christian life, Jesus prunes and removes the parts of us that do not bring us closer to Him. As with a vine, the only way the branch stays healthy is if it remains connected to that vine. When branches are removed from a tree, they die quickly because they are not receiving the life that comes from being connected to the source. In the same way, if we do not remain connected to our source, we face spiritual death. Our spiritual health decays, and we experience what it feels like to be apart from the eternal source of life. Jesus is, and will be, the only One who ever sustains us.

So, as you read these pages, figure out who you are today and who you want to be tomorrow. Do you want to be identified by a culture and society, or by the eternal identity that has been waiting for you? This world is constantly changing, and we cannot move our identity away from the only security we will ever have. We also cannot define our worth and our value from our past or from the issues we struggle with. Scripture says that all have fallen short of the glory **Know who you are and** of God, but, as was mentioned earli-**whose you are.** er, we have been made new. We have a new identity the moment we accept Christ, and it is the only unshakeable identity we will truly ever have.[6] Fads change, the world changes, our circumstances may change, but the God of the universe never

---

[5] 2 Corinthians 5:17
[6] Romans 3:23

does. The faster we anchor ourselves in that hope, the easier it is to reject identities we were never meant to have.

Know who you are and whose you are. With this weapon in your arsenal, you will have the strength to continue to fight the good fight of faith, even when hardships and difficulties come.

Discussion Questions

1. How have you identified yourself in the past?

_____

_____

_____

_____

2. How do you define yourself in light of the Gospel?

_____

_____

_____

_____

3. What does it mean to be adopted into God's royal family?

_____

_____

_____

_____

Chapter 4
IN THIS WORLD YOU WILL HAVE TROUBLE...

I learned at a very early age that hardship is a part of life. Through personal difficulty as well as watching the people around me, I learned that life is sometimes just flat tough. Scripture never said that life would be full of glitter and rainbows, but because of salvation, life is always full of hope. God has graciously provided us tools to be able to overcome, when times are difficult.

Aside from my aforementioned struggles with same-sex attraction, I also dealt with depression and eating disorders. Everything kind of hit the proverbial fan at the same time, and it left me reeling. I did not feel like I could control any part of my life, and I began making destructive choices when it came to my body. I did not treat it like it belonged to God but rather something that deserved punishment. My journey into an eating disorder was created by negative body image struggles and also driven by my lack of control of circumstances. I figured if I could not control anything else in my life, I could control what I put in my body. I did not know that my struggle would end up controlling me. Depression took me down a long path because I was trying to find my joy in places that would never be able to provide it. Depression is a real enemy, and it needs real help. During this period of my life, however, I was not trying to do anything to help it because I had gotten comfortable in my pain and figured there was nothing I could do to change what was happening. Again, my focus was on my circumstances when, the whole time, Jesus was right there waiting for me. I did not realize it because my focus was in the wrong place. I have learned that I do not always have control over difficult circumstances, but I do have control over how I respond and what I allow myself to take away from those circumstances. I just have to change my focus.

Coupled with everything else, a month before my high school graduation, my grandfather passed away. It was completely unexpected, and it rocked my family's world. This man had been an active part of my life for all of it. He was around before my parents met, and he did everything he could to take care of me. I was the only granddaughter, and with that came a special relationship. My grandpa was not perfect, but he was mine. I will never forget the day we had to say goodbye. It was honestly one of the worst days of my life and another of those moments that I had absolutely no control over. His passing was sudden because we had all expected that he would make a full recovery. There were times I was not sure how to recover from the grief of his death, but God in His goodness was already working this miserable situation into something that could be used for my good and His glory.

I know there are people out there who have had much more

difficult journeys. I know there are things people have experienced that I could not even begin to fathom. The stories I have heard working with teenagers in Teen Challenge have opened my eyes to pain I did not even know was possible. This sin-cursed world is full of so much difficulty and heartache, and it is hard to watch people struggle through their pain. However, no matter what your pain, you can overcome. I have learned that we all do ourselves a disservice when we compare our pain. I have heard numerous individuals say they did not want to share what was going on in their lives because it was not nearly as bad as what other people go through. Just like we are not meant to compare our successes in life to others, we are not meant to compare our pain. Pain looks different for everyone and still needs to be dealt with and brought into the loving arms of King Jesus. Any pain left undealt with can leave deep wounds that were not meant to be carried. This does not mean that we run around calloused to those around us. God gives us discernment to know when to share and when not to share, understanding that, no matter what, our only true place of healing is found with Jesus. While God can (and does) use those around us as His hands and feet, He will be the only one who can truly heal our broken hearts.

One of my favorite biblical examples of overcoming difficulty is the whole book of Esther. In her story, the lives of her people hang in the balance, and God has placed her in a position of leadership to be able to do something about it. If she approaches the King without his permission, she could lose her life. Esther did not always feel like she was able to complete the task before her. The man trying to annihilate the Jews was a man of high position and authority. However, Esther was able to overcome her fears and was granted divine favor. Esther should have lost her life the moment she entered the throne room without invitation, but she allowed God to use her. Her uncle Mordecai told her that she was in her position for such a time as this. Even though Esther was very much a human being with real concern for her life, her obedience led to a beautiful display of God's glory.

It does not take much to see the hardship facing our world today. Our news is riddled with stories of violence, confusion, and anger. In my work with Teen Challenge, the struggles that my girls faced were extremely heart-breaking. There are things adults, let alone thirteen-year-old girls, should never have to face. Behind the presenting issues my girls brought in were deeply-rooted hurts planted by shame, inadequacy, failure, and no idea that their heavenly Father loved them more than could ever imagine. I have worked with codependency, sexual identity struggles, anger, pornography, depression, suicide, drug abuse, and inappropriate sexual relationships to name a few. However, I have learned that underneath all those problems is a core issue of identity. Because of what these girls had done or been through, they identified themselves based on circumstances, poor choices, or hurts that they had experienced. Their struggles felt insurmountable. Of course, all our experiences have the power to shape us and influence how we approach different topics. Since I have struggled with same-sex attraction, I am able to broach the topic through the lens of what I have experienced. However, as was discussed earlier, I have learned that what shapes me is not what defines me. We can allow our hurts to teach us and mold us, but we cannot allow our hurts to identify us.

We can allow our hurts to teach us and mold us, but we cannot allow our hurts to identify us.

Too often, we define ourselves by the hardships we face. We feel trapped and irredeemable. We are told that we will face trials and temptation, but we are also told that we will be given a way to stand up under these trials. Trials do not identify us. Our identity is not meant to be found in the shaky foundations of failures, past hurts, or present struggle; our identity is meant to be found in the solid rock of Jesus Christ. Life can sometimes be just flat hard, and God understands this. Jesus himself was tempted and faced pain in ways that I will never be able to understand! We are not impervious beings who do not feel pain, but we are beings who have been given a Holy Spirit who intercedes for us and helps us in our weaknesses. Use the tools to create a solid foundation.[7]

As a teenager, I defined myself by my struggles. My troubles became my entire world, and I was bogged down by my thoughts. No matter what I did or how hard I tried, I just could not shake the pain. I let my mind run completely rampant and had not learned the importance of discipline in my thought life. I turned to eating disorders and cutting because I figured that if I could not control anything else in my world (or seemingly my mind), I could control what I was doing to myself. I felt unworthy and unlovable, so I treated myself accordingly. The interesting part about my emotionally-charged teenage rationale was that I could not see that everything I was trying to control ended up controlling me.

My high school years honestly seem like a blur and a far-distant memory. They are riddled with shame, fear, and a loss of true purpose and belonging. As I progressed through life, I experienced the loss of friendships that I thought would stay with me forever. I let people in and felt the impact of watching them walk away. However, I did not stay in that pain. I let go of the shaky foundation I had

---

[7] 1 Corinthians 10:13; Romans 8:26

created and planted myself in my God-given identity. I quit finding my validity in people and found it in the eyes of my Heavenly Father. The old expression that sticks and stones may break our bones, but words will never hurt us is just plain ridiculous. Of course, words and actions can hurt us, but no matter the pain, our story does not have to end there.

God gives us a choice. We can choose to let the troubles of this world destroy us, or we can let God's strength help us overcome. It is not an easy thing to overcome some of the situations in our lives. Though we are not always in control of what happens to us or around us, we are in control of how we frame experiences, how we learn from them, and how we choose to move forward. Some of those same girls that I talked about earlier went through some horrendous things. Instead of just continuing down that same destructive path, I watched several of these girls say that they were going to use their difficult times to help those around them.

If we allow Him to, God will be with us to help us overcome anything the world might throw our way.

Discussion Questions

1. What are some areas in your life where you are facing hardship?

_____

_____

_____

_____

2. How has this affected your life?

_____

_____

_____

_____

3. Do you want your struggles to be the defining factor in your life? Why or why not?

_____

_____

_____

_____

Chapter 5
BUT TAKE HEART! I HAVE OVERCOME THE WORLD

I have loved Disney movies for as long as I can remember, and I love that good always triumphs over evil. Even from an early age, most of us were exposed to the concept of darkness, but we knew that it was always meant to be overcome. Prince Eric gets rid of Ursula in The Little Mermaid; Cinderella still gets to marry the prince despite her step-mother's attempts; Snow White gets awakened by true love's kiss after eating one nasty apple; the Beast discovers how to truly love, and he and Belle live happily ever after—I think we get the point. Our world likes to see stories where good triumphs over evil. Of course, we as Christians know that the ultimate triumph came over 2,000 years ago at Calvary and allows us to live in freedom today.

It took me a long time to realize that God could and would help me overcome every obstacle I had ever faced as a teenager.

When you deal with something for so long, and especially in silence, it makes it seem like an insurmountable mountain that is just waiting to constantly topple you over. We forget the victory is already there and feel bogged down by one insane weight. It is hard to know where to begin because it seems that there is just too much to tackle, but Scripture offers hope. This is another reason why I am such a proponent of biblical counseling. It has been such a comfort in my own life to be able to sit across from someone who I know truly believes that Jesus is the only way to overcome and helps me see the blind spots in my life. Sometimes it just takes a listening ear to help see where to begin the long and arduous process. There is power when we allow Christ to be the central part of our healing. Without Him, we are left with the strength within, which taps out quickly.

Understanding Christ to be the center of my process to overcome my struggles has led to several pivotal moments. As I continue to grow, the pivotal moments continue to come. From sharing with my friend Alina about my struggles, to now spending lots of time researching the ways we wire our brain to think, I am having new aspects of God's grace and mercy revealed to me daily. While it might take time and determination, overcoming can and will happen. God gives us the ability to win.

Part of overcoming life-controlling struggles is understanding that we have a choice. We have a choice in what we allow ourselves to think about, what we believe, and what we allow to be the overall narrative in our lives. This very concept of choice seems to sometimes be lost on our current society. I am not a neuroscientist, but I have been intrigued by the work of Dr. Caroline Leaf. I have mentioned her before, and that is because she is brilliant. She profoundly breaks down the ways our brains think and how we do indeed have the ability to destroy (not just push aside) the toxic thought patterns in our brains. Her book "Switch On Your Brain" does a fantastic job of unpacking this life-changing process. We do get to change what we think about.[8]

Another part of overcoming negative thought patterns and hardship is choosing to put in the hard work. Unfortunately, we live in a society marked by entitlement and instant gratification. Anything that requires a little sweat and brain power is far from appealing. However, I have come to realize that I learn more as I engage every aspect of the healing and overcoming process. No one can do the hard work for us, and no one can make us turn our lives around or remove ourselves from a negative situation. Most of my girls came to Teen Challenge because they had to. For many of them, it took several months to even decide that they had things in their lives that needed to change. For others, they never made that choice and just went through the motions until they could leave the program. We live in a world where we want others to do the hard stuff. Digging up past hurt and acknowledging areas of our lives that need change is not fun. While I have found great healing through the process of counseling and through loving people who tell me when I need to get my act together, it has never been something that I have deemed as fun. However, as I look back over my life, where I am today would be completely different had I not made the choice to put in the hard work. God is with us, and God equips us, but God is not going to make us do anything. We are given free will and have the ability to do with it whatever we want. God is not sitting up in heaven controlling our every step or pulling the strings on our little

---

[8] Leaf, Caroline. *Switch On Your Brain: The Key To Peak Happiness and Health.* Grand Rapids, Mich.: Baker Books, 2013.

puppets. God will help us, but we must make the choice to want to help ourselves.

Christians struggle, and I have had my fair share of those struggles. On top of learning that good little church girls have difficulty and struggle just like everyone else, I have learned that good little church girls have choices. We get to choose our level of victory. It has already been given to us, but we have to choose to accept it. We have to choose to change our minds and our outlook. Sometimes, we have to choose to remove ourselves from a bad situation. We will never be able to truly overcome if we never acknowledge we have a part to play. Grab a hold of the freedom that God so desperately desires for you. But understand that He will never force it on you.

Through the cross of Jesus Christ, we are overcomers. His Spirit gives us the strength to say no to the flesh and yes to the Spirit. Just because we all have a sin nature does not mean that we have to be ruled by it. We need to choose. Choose this day who you will serve.[9] God commanded Israel to choose because they kept messing around with idols and false gods. We are told the same thing today. Choose if you are going to live subject to your pain for the rest of your life. Choose if you are going to live defined by past mistakes or hardships. Choose who you are going to serve. It is in our weaknesses that Christ's strength is made perfect. As a counselor, I have had the privilege of seeing people who have proven that the willingness to put in the work and reliance on God allows for true change. This principle does not mean perfection is achieved, because sanctification is an ongoing process. It does mean that we learn, and we allow the Holy Spirit to equip us to move into a better tomorrow. God is a

---

[9] Joshua 24:15

44

good God, and He desires our good. We should choose Him.

God shows His goodness in multiple ways, and one of the ways He is teaching me His grace is through my precious niece. Children have a way of making you either utterly insane or completely mushy because of all the cute things they can do. Every time my niece sees me and gets a larger-than-life smile on her face coupled with such uncontainable excitement, everything else in life just melts away. No matter how difficult my day might have been or how tired I might be, that little girl has the power to change my perspective just because she unashamedly loves me. She does not love me because I buy her little fox xylophones or am trying to covertly implant thoughts of Disney bliss in her head; she loves me because she knows me. She allows me to hold her because she trusts me. She knows that I love her (and, let's be real, she knows I am completely wrapped around every one of those adorable little fingers of hers). In the same regard, I know my Heavenly Father loves me. When Christ chose to hang on the cross at Calvary, He chose to redeem every hurtful thing I would do and every mistake I would make because He loves me. And why does He love me? Because He knows me. Because He knows I am His kid, and there is nothing in this world that could ever take that away. He loves me enough to pick me back up when I have a misstep.

I have fallen on my face more times than I would ever like to count. I have hurt people in ways I wish I never would have. I have made so many mistakes. But no matter what, I know my Heavenly Father is looking down and smiling. When I enter His presence, He surrounds me with peace and an inexplicable feeling of true joy because He knows what I often forget: in Him, every trouble will melt away.

45

This does not mean that we get to make the choice to keep on deliberately sinning. True repentance and true understanding of our Heavenly Father's love for us leads to a complete 180 in how we are often walking through life. God understands that we are not perfect, but again, we still get to choose. We get to choose if we want to keep living in a lifestyle that has become comfortable to us or if we want to go through the hard work to allow God to take back His rightful place as the King of our lives. Earlier I talked about my very skewed mentality of believing that because I was a good church girl, I was never going to encounter hardship or make stupid choices. Of course, I now understand that this is so unbelievably far from the truth. But, I also understand that I get to choose how I want to move forward from those mistakes and what I want to be my defining moments. We have such a beautiful example of what it means to walk through difficulty and be an overcomer, and that is through none other than Jesus.

Jesus was no stranger to difficulty and suffered through more pain and heartache than I will ever know. However, He knew that the victory would always and forever ultimately be His. The victory in our lives is the same. We can take comfort in knowing that our pain, our heartache, our trouble will one day pass away, and, until that moment, God will give us the strength to carry on. When we feel like we have no fight left, God will fight for us. God also understands that when we make a choice to let Him be the victorious King, we will need lots of help. He understands that we cannot do it on our own. When we allow Him to be a part of the process, He will graciously always be there.

Now, when you or someone you know is struggling, please do me a favor. Please do not tell them that they need to pray about that or ask them how often they have. Believe me, I am a FIRM believer in the power of prayer, and I know that prayer works. However, when those phrases are stated, it can often have a negative impact and make the other individual feel as if what they are going through can be easily dismissed. On top of that, if they are God-honoring, God-fearing people, they have probably taken the time to pray about it. However, God's ways are higher than our ways, and we cannot always understand or immediately see how our negative situation can be turned into a positive one. Often, we face hardship because of poor choices or actions, but other times, we face hardship because we live in a sin-stained and broken world. So yes, we do have a choice to make a change, but we also have a choice to meet people right where they are.

When people are hurting (and I am speaking about this from first-hand experience), they don't want **Empathy goes a long** a 30-step guide to the prayers that will fix **way when helping** their lives. When people are hurting, **someone who is truly** they want your ear, your hug, and your heart. Em- **struggling.** pathy goes a long way when helping someone who is truly struggling. Does this mean we let people just skate by and live recklessly? Of course not. What it does mean is that we have developed enough of a relationship with, and are close enough to, Jesus that we will follow His promptings instead of our own fleshly ones. Often, people can come to a conclusion that helps them see what steps to take in order to move forward in a healthy direction. However, this discernment does not come due to human wisdom or well-intentioned advice but through Holy Spirit promptings and direction.

So how can we approach someone who is hurting? The same way we would want to approach anyone: with love, empathy, and a

47

sensitive spirit. When I have been in hard places, people have called me on the carpet, but they also made sure to tell me how much they loved me, and they believed in me. When people are hurting, they have generally beaten themselves down enough in some way, shape, or form, so we don't need to add another hammer. God convicts; we serve in obedience. Be willing to love, and, when the time comes, let God lead you in sharing the necessary truths.

Working with teenagers who have faced crazy things has taught me that, more than anything, people just want to know that someone loves them unconditionally. No matter how many foolish things my girls did, they knew that I loved them. Now, I loved them enough to get in their faces, but I also loved them enough to let them know that in and through Christ there is nothing that cannot be overcome. We are told in Scripture that the Spirit intercedes for us with groanings too deep for words.[10] How powerful!

There is also something to be said of attitude. We get the beautiful opportunity to affect how we perceive a situation (I am speaking to myself here, too), and we also get to choose how we react to it. In case you are not catching a pattern here, choice plays a huge role. A dear friend of mine often encourages me when I am feeling troubled to just spend time in worship, in prayer, and just continuously thanking God. Why do we do this in the middle of a hardship or a difficulty? Because it takes our minds off the problem and puts them right back on Jesus. When we shift our mindset back onto our Creator it does not necessarily change the situation, but it changes how we are able to respond and move forward. When we look at life through the lens of Christ, it changes how we respond,

---

[10] Romans 8:26

how we think, and how we ultimately move forward.

The same neuroscientist I mentioned earlier, Dr. Caroline Leaf, has a beautiful program called the 21-Day Brain Detox that addresses this very aspect. In her work, she encourages each of those walking through the program to begin with thanksgiving, praise and worship. When we put God at the center of our minds and of our lives, we invite Him to truly speak into our hearts. It is hard to hear God when our minds are full of clutter. I am one who can completely understand what it means to have a mind full of clutter. It is so easy to focus on everything around us. When we do this, we have a harder time allowing ourselves the wonderful privilege of just being in communion with our Creator.[11] Does this mean things are not any harder? No, but it means we have invited Jesus to walk alongside us, and we ultimately know that He is the One who is on our side and will be the One who changes how we are able to think, feel and respond in the middle of life's biggest difficulties. There is something **No matter your pain, no matter how insurmountable that mountain might seem, Jesus has overcome.** to be said for counting it ALL joy, as it says in James 1:2.

So, if you are hurting today, take heart because Jesus has overcome the world. No matter your pain, no matter how insurmountable that mountain might seem, Jesus has overcome. And another beautiful thing about it? God helps us by not making us overcome alone.

---

[11] Leaf, Caroline. *Switch On Your Brain: The Key To Peak Happiness and Health.* Grand Rapids, Mich.: Baker Books, 2013.

Discussion Questions

1. What are ways that you can overcome the hardships in your life?

_____

_____

_____

_____

2. In light of understanding your own ability to overcome, how can you encourage others who are struggling to do the same?

_____

_____

_____

_____

3. How can you claim victory in your life?

_____

_____

_____

_____

Chapter 6
THE ARMY THAT WON'T STOP GROWING

I know everyone says this, but I seriously have the best support network in the whole wide world. Every crazy (or seemingly crazy) idea I have had has been supported and encouraged and, most importantly, bathed in prayer. Isolation is a scary place to be, and it is never a place we were meant to be. Life is meant to be done in tandem with others. Galatians tells us to bear one another's burdens for a reason, but there are a million reasons why we do not.[12]

Sometimes, being alone is easier than the fear of being rejected. When we are really going through the pits, we are often afraid of what others might do, say, or think. But, God created us to be the body for a reason. We are meant to do life in tandem for a reason. If we feel like we are alone on a desert island, it is much harder to un-

---

[12] Galatians 6:2

derstand that there are people who relate to us and understand some of the things we have walked through. It is much easier to listen to reason when we are in a place where our voice is not the only one we hear. Community is a vital part of our success.

God uses people as tangible expressions of His love and mercy, and I am fortunate to have some of the best expressions out there. Beginning at age eighteen, I have had several people positively impacting my journey and helping me understand not only who I am but whose I am. The friends I have all entered at the perfect moment, and God has used them to teach me some valuable lessons. My introverted friends all laugh because I basically forced them to be friends with me (not really, but I just enjoy a good, dramatic story sometimes). There is something encouraging about knowing you have people walking with you no matter what.

When I get married, I know that God will use my husband to encourage me and challenge me. But, through a series of hard life moments, I have learned that people cannot be my everything. I have fallen into the trap of making people the ones who fulfill my every need instead of Jesus more times than I can count. The beautiful part of a godly army is knowing that it grows and is centered around a relationship with Christ, which means I know Christ is the One who truly keeps the army going. God-honoring relationships are the best ones because they keep the focus right where it should be: on Jesus. God-honoring friends are the ones who love you enough to tell you the hard stuff and tell you when you are being ridiculous. They are the ones who laugh with you, cry with you, and push you to be everything that God has for you. They are the ones who will go to war with you and for you.

Some of the people in my army are defenders, which I basically interpret as "come at anyone I love, bro. I dare you." They fight hard for the ones they love and do not allow people to act a fool around them. God fights for us, too. He stands against the enemy on our behalf and makes sure the Devil knows he has no dominion over God's chosen ones. God loves us enough to tell us the truth and loves us enough to fight for us. I get to see tangible expressions of this beautiful picture daily.

I see an army as a unit that looks out for the needs of their fellow soldiers. They are trained to take a bullet (sometimes literally) for those they fight with and understand that working as a team is critically important to the mission. As the body of Christ, we are our own army. Each of us has an integral part to play, and it can harm the rest of the body if we do not step into the role that God designed us for. In a war, if someone steps out on their own, ignoring the needs of their unit or not following orders, it can mean life or death. It is important to understand that an army can be an unstoppable force if each soldier plays the role they were meant to play. Each person in my army plays an integral, but different, part in my life. They all challenge me in different ways, but they are ultimately about the same goal as I am — seeing God's glory made known.

This incredible network I have is spread all over the country, but they each act as a tangible reminder of **God places people in our lives to be important parts of our journey.** the faithfulness of God. God was even so kind as to bring one member of my army back into my life from the recesses of my childhood. It is amazing to me how God orchestrates each event so beautifully. God knows who we need and when we need them. It is important to understand that we do not rely on this army to be our everything. But, we do know that God places people in our lives to be important parts of our journey.

One of the most beautiful examples, to me, of friendship is not found in Taylor Swift's squad, but in King David and Jonathan. I am sure most of us are familiar with this story, but, just in case you are not, allow me to give you a quick snapshot. King David and Jonathan had a very unlikely friendship because David seemingly took Jonathan's rightful place as King of Israel. Jonathan's dad was the infamous King Saul, and Jonathan should have been the next in line. However, due to his father's choices, God's anointing shifted from King Saul onto a shepherd boy named David who killed a giant with three little stones. Jonathan had a choice to make of whether he would allow this moment to change how he viewed his relationship with David.

Jonathan could have hated David, but he did not. He not only honored David as the rightful heir apparent to the throne of Israel, but he protected him however he could. He sacrificed a position of power and influence to be a man of obedience. This is a lesson we could all learn. Jonathan loved David as his own brother. He died before he was able to see David become a great king, but Scripture shows the lasting impact Jonathan had on David. One of the most beautiful parts of this story, to me, is that because of who Jonathan was in David's life, David honored his family well beyond Jonathan's mortal life. In most royal lines, the conquering King was sure to remove the remaining heirs of the previous line to make sure that a revolt or mutiny did not happen. But, this was not the case for David. He honored his friend because of the level of honor and sacrifice his friend had shown him. This is a beautiful representation of what a godly friendship looks like.[13]

[13] 1 Samuel 18:1-6; 20; 2 Samuel 9

I don't know about you, but I want those kinds of friend-ships in my army. I want people who will walk in obedience and will help me be the woman of God I am supposed to be. I want peo-ple who will tell me the hard stuff because they want to see me be the best version of myself but will do so in love and grace. You can be straightforward, but you can also be straightforward with tact. I have a friend who, in the last year, really opened my eyes to a blind spot I was experiencing. She was direct, but man, I knew that she was speaking out of a place of love and not wanting me to keep walking crippled. Her honesty led me on a huge path of redirecting my focus and rewiring my mind. I will forever be grateful that she took the time to love me and to love me in a godly way. These are the kinds of friendships and relationships that can catapult us forward into a life of great and godly purpose.

Some of you reading this book might be introverted, which just means you recharge being by yourself. I am not saying that you need to completely shift your personality type to enjoy being around people 24/7 like I do. Just know that God did not intend for you to live life alone. Your circle might be small, and that is okay. Just find the people to have in your life who are going to lead you closer to Jesus. Find people who appreciate the unique ways that God has created and gifted you. Isolation is, in my opinion, one of the biggest tactics that the enemy uses against us. Be mindful of his tricks, and know that life is meant to be done in community. It is great if you are selective, and if you aren't, I encourage you to be a little more so. Our business is not for the Facebook world to see or for every person on planet earth to understand. But, I do believe that there are individuals out there who will continue to encourage you to be the person God has created you to be.

In case you have not caught on, I absolutely love Disney movies and could watch them on repeat. I am convinced that Disney is my rightful home here on this earth, and I would love to just permanently live on the property even though that would surely mean I would go entirely broke. The whole point of my tangent is to point you to another Disney film that I thoroughly enjoy because it is not only about a princess finding her prince, but also about the princesses' finding each other. The movie Frozen is unlike any other Disney film in that it places the emphasis on the relationships between Princess Anna and Princess Elsa. These two sisters go on a journey to discover that true love was not in some man that they met five seconds ago but in the love they had for one another — a sisterly love. (Sorry if you have not seen the movie, major spoiler alert). We are all siblings through the blood of Jesus Christ, and it is important that we connect with and sharpen one another. I love how Scripture speaks of ironing sharpening iron, and that a brother loves at all times and a friend is born for adversity.[14]

When we understand that people will fail us, whether it is intentional or not, it will be much easier to understand that these people in our lives are not meant to function as our perfect Creator. Healthy friendships are not always conflict-free, but that's because we are learning how to become more Christ-like every day. Healthy friendships are also not anchored in another person but anchored in the Cross of Jesus Christ. Just because God gives us friends or a spouse does not mean we expect them to take on a role that only God was intended to fill. People will fail us, and we cannot allow those expe-

---

[14] Proverbs 17:17

riences to shape how we view our Heavenly Father. His love for us is perfect, and the people in our lives will always be imperfect. When we understand that people will fail us, whether it is intentional or not, it will be much easier to understand that these people in our lives are not meant to function as our perfect Creator.

I have alluded to codependency at other points in this book, but again, it basically just means that all our emotional needs are placed in another person's basket, whether that's a spouse or friend. It means one's world rises and falls with a particular individual, and that dependency leads to a great level of toxicity in a relationship. Many abusive relationships stem from codependent ones because the codependent individual finds their entire worth and value in another person. They cannot think, move, live, or breathe without the other person. This is not a healthy picture of the army God intends for us to have. Godly people were always meant to be extensions of God's love but never the source. One of the aforementioned members of my army has also always told me to approach my friendships with open hands. This means we allow them to be who God intends them to be without trying to con-**Do not ever allow yourself** trol how people will respond to **to define a perfect Creator** us. Some of my friends have been **by His imperfect, fallen** around for a long time, and others have moved on or **creation.** just recently come on the scene, but because I know they are not my source, I trust that God will bring the people I need when I need them. And He has.

Do not ever allow yourself to define a perfect Creator by His imperfect, fallen creation. We are meant to do life in community, but this does not mean our community will not hurt us. If they are God-loving people, they will do what they can to make amends and

57

move forward. But, sometimes even the most God-fearing people do things that boggle our minds. If we keep in mind that our armies are extensions of God Himself, we will understand that even if hurt comes, we can keep moving forward. As I mentioned earlier, healthy friendships can (and often do) have some level of conflict. Each person functions in different ways, and, no matter how similar our personalities might be, we are all unique. Learning how to love one another takes intentionality, and it also takes grace. The more we approach life knowing who our source is, the easier it is to appreciate friendships for the gifts that they are. When we find these extensions of God's love and mercy, we also find a powerful place to bring our greatest darkness into redeeming light.

Discussion Questions

1. Who are you allowing to influence your life? Are they positive influences or negative influences?

   _____

   _____

   _____

   _____

2. Who are you choosing to anchor your life in?

   _____

   _____

   _____

   _____

3. What kinds of friendships do you want to have?

   _____

   _____

   _____

   _____

Chapter 7

POWER IN THE LIGHT

One of the most magical moments of my entire life was setting foot in the Magic Kingdom at Walt Disney World. For us Disney fanatics, those castles are almost a beacon calling us home. (You might think that's ridiculous, but really, go experience it). Disney knows how to make you feel like royalty the moment you set foot on the property, and they also know how to put on a show. At the end of every night, each park puts on a firework show, and let me tell you, it does not disappoint. No matter where you are in the park, you can see those lights, and it is a sign that you need to get to where the action is. I think I enjoy the lights of these parks so much because they remind me of Christmas. During the Christmas season, it is one of my greatest joys to be able to drive around and look at all the twinkly lights hung on people's houses. Light offers hope. It's the one speck of bright on a cold and dreary December night. Light opens our eyes to whole new possibilities. Light also exposes things for what they really are.

I got the chance to travel all over Florida with one of my best friends, and while there, we got to go see the historic lighthouse of St. Augustine. Lighthouses serve as a signal to those out at sea that land is close. At St. Augustine, men ran up and down several flights of stairs carrying heavy buckets of oil to make sure that light was always shining. I have to believe their work was exhausting, but I cannot even imagine the relief of any sailor that came upon these towers. No matter what their journey had been, they were now close to home. Lighthouses expose the nearness of land, but they also beckon sailors into the light and call them home. Light offers hope.

The Gospel does the exact same thing; it calls us out of our **No matter what our** mess, brings us home, and gives us hope. **journeys have been or how** No matter what our journeys **many storms we have** have been or how many storms we **encountered, we can rest** have encountered, we can rest on **on the shores of God's** the shores of God's grace. The Gos- **grace.** pel message allows the darkest spaces of our hearts to be exposed to the light and truth of God's mercy and grace. We understand that through the cross, all our failures, all our shame, and all our heartache is redeemed through the blood of Christ.

Darkness often causes stumbling because we cannot see where we are going. I am prone to klutziness, and being in the dark does not help my cause. Any time the lights are off in my house, I am guaranteed to trip over the tiniest cord (or even the air). However, the moment the light comes on, it shows me what I could not see before: the pesky cord that is secretly out to get me. There are also moments when we move that piece of furniture that has been in the exact same spot for the last several years only to discover the earring we lost in junior high or the tootsie roll our family members magically seemed to misplace. We can uncover the forgotten things or the stuff that now just needs to be thrown away because light has shown what was covered. We can only see what has been brought into the light. When we accept the message of salvation, the metaphorical light comes on, and we can see all the areas of our lives that had been hiding in the darkness. They become exposed and can be changed, or if necessary, removed.

Bringing anything into the light requires a level of vulnerability that is not always comfortable. We all know the sensation of being in the dark and having lights come on without warning. Squinty eyes are a real thing, and it is often accompanied by lots of groaning noises. When we have been sitting in darkness, light is not comfortable, but it does allow us to see the world around us. Light exposes the toilet paper that has been hung all over people's trees (I hope tee-peeing is still a thing, or I am feeling older than I should), or the trash that we let pile up from that oh-so-exciting overnighter. Light exposes the areas of our lives that need to be cleaned up, and, while it is not always fun, the end result of exposure to the light is well worth the effort.

What happens if we allow stinky trash to stay where it is or toilet paper to be strewn all over the trees and yard? It becomes a much worse problem. Often, this is how sin ends up invading our lives. We leave our mess in the dark and allow it to grow into something much greater than it was ever intended to be. But, when the light comes on, and we accept the grace that comes with God's salva-

Bringing anything into the light requires a level of vulnerability that is not always comfortable.

tion, we see where we need to change. Thankfully, the beauty of the Gospel is that we do not have to attempt change alone. Jesus is right there with the metaphorical trash bag ready to help us clean up the mess.

The more often I shared my testimony and allowed myself to be vulnerable, the less scary my giant became. When the flashlight was turned on my struggle, that giant started to shrink away until it pretty much altogether dissipated. In my head, the struggle was always a looming giant and would never go away. With the light of Jesus, it was exposed as something that truly had no power and no place in my life. Now, this does not mean it felt like rainbows and butterflies the first time the Holy Spirit prompted me to share my struggle. In fact, I remember the distinct sensation of wanting to throw up, curl into a ball, and run away all at the same time. However, the more I shared, the more I felt Jesus wrap His loving arms around me and give me peace. The more I shared, the more I saw that my looming giant was something that had already been placed under the blood of Jesus and only had power over me because I was the one allowing it to have the power.

Not everyone has received my testimony well, but that is not what shining the light is truly about. Sharing my testimony opened my heart up to the possibility that my life could be so much more than what I had made it be and that people could love me despite the darkest parts of me. It allowed me the opportunity to experience healing, peace, and, ultimately, joy that I never even knew was possible. It has bridged gaps in ways that I did not even imagine and given me more chances to speak truth to a world that desperately needs to hear it. People everywhere are struggling, and there is something about knowing that you are not the only one who faces what you face. Not everyone struggles in the same ways that I do, but we all have our stuff, and we all have the dark places in our hearts that no one gets to shine a light on. Though it may be scary, the important part is to allow in light that eradicates fear, doubt, and anxiety. The truth of who God is and the light of the Gospel message do not allow the enemy any ability to stand.

When I was a kid, I hated the dark (if I'm going to be real, I'm still not a big fan of it unless I can hear ocean waves, or I am sitting at a bonfire eating S'mores). My grandpa, God bless him, felt the need to buy me expensive and creepy dolls that I could have SWORN were staring at me as I slept. When I would run to my mom's and dad's room, there would be one of these oh-so-lovely dolls looming over my head as it sat atop their entertainment center. However, in the light of the day, those dolls were shown for exactly what they were. They were not the boogey man waiting to terrorize me or some weird Chucky doll; they were just porcelain dolls that were gifted to me out of the kindness of my grandfather's heart. Looking at these dolls in light of that truth made looking at them less scary when the lights were not on.

In the dark, our struggles can look really scary. They can loom over us and cause us to want to revert to that child-like state of running for the hills. However, the moment we turn that metaphorical light on, we see these struggles for what they really are. We see the truth that God is much bigger than anything our enemy could throw at us. Eventually, the issue loses its power because we recognize it for what it is; a lie that has been conquered through the blood of Jesus Christ. This understanding that Jesus has already conquered those lies does not mean that overcoming our struggles is a seamless process, but it does mean that there is power and ability to remove these dark places from our lives.

Let me give just a few other examples of what the power of the light will do. I have alluded to the fact that the Holy Spirit has prompted me on more than one occasion to share about my struggles with same-sex attraction, but allow me to break down how those moments and the light that they gave truly brought healing to my life. The impact these experiences have continues to shape me, and God continues to use them in my work with other people. Now, I am so thankful for what each of these experiences has taught me.

While I was in college, God prompted me yet again to share my struggle, but this time, it was going to be in chapel to a room full of girls. The campus pastor at Evangel University (located in lovely Springfield, Missouri, for those not familiar) had graciously offered me the opportunity to share at an evening chapel, but the topic was one I was far from comfortable with. The crazy thing is, my campus pastor let me preach whatever I wanted to, but what God wanted me to share made me more uncomfortable than I was willing to let on. Again, I reverted to that thought process of wondering what these people would think if they knew what I struggled with and what the darkest places of my heart looked like. People knew I was called into full-time ministry, and I wondered if my monstrous giant would taint their image of me. However, God used my obedience, and that chapel ended up having a very positive impact on both me and the people I shared my story with. My senior year of college was a stretching year all the way around, but God was so gracious each time the door was opened for me to share some of the most vulnerable places of my heart.

Before I felt okay to share to that room full of girls, I knew I needed to share with two very important people in my army. I did not want to tell them any more than I wanted to share the first time three years earlier. I distinctly remember spending lots of time spinning around in a chair and hiding in my thick, curly hair mop to avoid eye contact. I was clammy, and I felt like a complete heel. However, they encouraged me and walked with me. They loved me, they hugged me, and they pushed me to keep moving forward. The other ironic thing is that all these individuals whom I told already knew what I struggled with. The Holy Spirit had spoken to them ahead of time on my behalf. I don't think this happens every time, and it would have made my life much easier if I had known that they already had a clue of what was coming. But, each time I shared, I felt more peace. I continued to gain an understanding that my struggle did not define me, and God showed me I am loveable. I healed through loving arms, encouraging words, and the ability to be open. All of this is a reminder that God cares about us enough to illuminate the areas in our lives that need healing. He wants our ultimate good for His glory.

During that same period, I shared with my college advisor what I had been through, and she spoke words that I never thought I would hear: "Oh, honey, if that would have happened to me at fourteen, it would have messed with me, too. You are NORMAL." I'm what? Normal. These were words I could not imagine even remotely ringing true in my life. I did not realize that an experience in the middle of my adolescence could be deemed as normal. None of these individuals told me to give into my feelings and to just run full force down the path of destruction. However, they understood that to be human is to struggle, and that to be a Christian is to find true and godly freedom. God used my senior year of college to really begin teaching me something: I struggled, but my struggle did not

67

have to be something that debilitated me, nor did it have to be what defined me. I struggled, but that did not mean people could not love me.

During my college career, I had the opportunity to go on several different mission's trips. One of these trips was to the Eastern European country of Romania. The mountains there are absolutely breathtaking, and Dracula's castle is not as scary when there are not vampires wandering around in it. While on this trip, I met a girl who quickly became one of my best friends and a formidable voice in my journey. She helped me choose my next steps and understand how God could continue to use my life and my story. She and I instantly bonded and spent the night in the same hotel room one evening. For several hours, we both poured out our hearts underneath weird bamboo décor and weird lighting. As I shared my story with her, it opened the door for her vulnerability. You see, when we can be real about the dark places of our own hearts, it helps others feel the liberty to do the same. So, we shared, we cried, we laughed, we overslept our alarms, and we healed. My friend Steph was the one who encouraged me to go on to grad school to get a counseling degree, and she continues to cheer me on as God opens doors. I had no clue that following the prompting of the Holy Spirit would open the doors it has, but that is what faith does; it opens doors to things we could never dream, hope, or imagine on our own.

In the book of Matthew, we are told that we are the light of the world, a city on a hill.[15] We get the unique opportunity to carry hope into a very lost and dying world. Light does not always illuminate pretty scenes, but it does give an opportunity to see things as

---

[15] Matthew 5:14

they really are. There is power in the light. It is not always comfortable, and it is not something many of us always enjoy. However, it is liberating. The army I spoke of earlier is an awesome tool that God uses to expose the dark places of our hearts. It is a safe place to begin the healing process. When we understand that Jesus did not die for us to sit in darkness unable to see where our hope truly lies, we can begin to pull back the metaphorical shades to let His light invade.

This process can often be a clunky one, and that is okay. As with learning any new skill, allowing the light takes practice and the willingness to try. I have people sit in my counseling office and let the light shine on some pretty scary and dust-covered areas of their lives. There is definitely a level of discomfort, and it does not feel like a smooth process. But, every time I have found that their level of willingness to shine a Holy Spirit flashlight on their darkness allows for an even greater opportunity of healing. Again, we get to have the choice. We get to choose whether we allow God to expose our darkness for what it really is. We get to choose whether we get to experience complete and God-given healing. We get to choose.

So, where are the areas of your life that need that light? We are all quite good at putting away certain aspects of our lives because hiding is much easier than dealing with the issue. However, we should not live in darkness. We **Put those Gospel gloves** were intended to live lives free of **on and let the message of** guilt, shame, and condemnation, **hope clean up what has** where we can walk in the light of t h e **been sitting in the** truth. Maybe as you're reading **darkness for far too long.** these pages, you're feeling the Holy Spirit gently nudge you to shine a light. I promise, as scary as it may be, there is a whole new level of freedom waiting for you today. Put those Gospel gloves on and let the message of hope clean up what has been sitting in the darkness for far too long. When we have the courage to bring what lays in darkness into light, we can have the power to let it go.

Discussion Questions

1. What light can the Gospel shine on the darkness of your life?

   _____

   _____

   _____

   _____

2. What areas of your life need to be exposed to the light?

   _____

   _____

   _____

   _____

3. Who are the people you can be vulnerable with?

   _____

   _____

   _____

   _____

Chapter 8
LET IT GO

If you are now singing Frozen songs and pretending you are Queen Elsa on a snow-covered mountain with a super cool ice palace because of the title of this chapter, you are welcome. No, seriously, I hope you can forgive me if you absolutely hate that song or have been made to listen to it by some excited four-year-old way more than you ever wanted to. I am that girl that loves to shout it out at the top of my lungs and makes all her friends hate it so much. I also do not have the excuse of being some cute four-year-old girl because pushing thirty is not quite the same. However, I love it.

One of the best pieces of advice I have ever been given is to quit giving my negative thoughts legs, which essentially means, let them go. We may not be able to control much in our lives, but we are able to control what we think about and dwell on. In Scripture, we are told that we have the ability to renew our mind.[16] Dr. Caroline

Leaf does an amazing job of teaching her readers how they can wire out every negative thought they have wired in. God did not design our brains to just be stuck in a state of distress, as this has a detrimental effect on our entire person.[17] In fact, He intended for our minds to be ruled by peace.

My personality type is one that likes to dwell. I am capable of sitting and stewing on something for so long that I lose multiple hours in the day before I even realize how long I have been thinking. I beat myself to a pulp (not literally, but you get the idea) wondering why things went wrong or why a situation has turned out like it has. Any form of feedback causes long, drawn out periods of thinking that are sometimes not even remotely necessary. However, I know that I am inclined to dwell for forever. This is not a healthy pattern because my dwelling often leads to torment and distress instead of dwelling on the Author of peace.

As I just implied, dwelling can really get me into some serious trouble. I am really good at creating situations and scenarios in my head before they have even happened because I am trying to anticipate the hurt before it comes. If I can beat the person or the situation to the proverbial punch, I can save myself more pain and heartache later down the road. I can get myself so worked up over the "what-ifs" that I completely lose sight of what actually is and cause myself much more stress than I ever intended. Analyzing the possible outcomes of a situation is one thing, but expecting the very worst out of everything that comes my way is a completely different story. Overall, this way of thinking is absolutely exhausting, causes

---

[16] Romans 12:2
[17] Leaf, Caroline. *Switch On Your Brain: The Key To Peak Happiness and Health.* Grand Rapids, Mich.: Baker Books, 2013.

my head to hurt, and makes me a little bit crabby! I have spent so much time focusing on the what-ifs, making me lose sight of present realities. While it is good to think through situations and how to best approach them, dwelling on the negative (or what could be the negative) puts us in a place where we are more apt to cause harm than good. Experience can be a powerful tool in learning how to deal with difficult situations, but we are not designed to think about the absolute worst every time we have a little bit of conflict in our lives.

One of my favorite Scripture verses is found in Isaiah, and it says that God keeps in perfect peace him whose mind is stayed on Him.[18] If I have learned anything about our enemy the Devil, it is that he is smart. He knows if he can keep us focused on our external circumstances instead of our eternal Creator, he can have an absolute hey-day with our minds. Satan does not desire for us to understand peace, let alone live in it. We are not going to be able to find peace in the latest fad, diet, or self-help book. We are going to find peace in centering our minds on Jesus. My favorite books to read are those that help others understand that help comes from the Creator. God uses people as His instruments, but we can only really let go through the power of Christ.

The Bible was penned by several different men, which is a prime example of how God uses His creation. However, these moments of brilliance we find in Scripture were not inspired by human intellect, but instead by Holy Spirit direction. Every thought-provoking moment I have had is not because some person is the most brilliant person in the whole wide world (though there are brilliant people out there), but because their brilliance is a gift that God uses

---

[18] Isaiah 26:3

to offer wisdom and insight into situations that I might not have had a solid understanding of before. Peace comes from God, and chaos comes from the enemy; we get to choose what we will grab a hold of and what we will let go.

Something that drives me absolutely crazy is blaming the Devil for our bad decisions. Satan does not cause us to make bad choices, nor does he make us dwell on things. He might throw the seed our direction, but we get to choose what we do with the thought and what actions we get to take. 2 Corinthians 10:5 tells us to take our thoughts captive and make them obedient to Christ, and this principle really works. God would not have said it if we could not do it. The Bible is the only infallible peace of literature this world will ever have because it con-tinues to stand the test of time as the inspired Word of God. We do not control every fleeting thought that pops into our heads, but you better believe we get to control what **Dwelling without action** we hold onto. When we allow our**leads to apathy.** selves to sit in a place of negativity, our whole perspective changes. We have got to learn to let things go.

Sometimes, we will be in messy situations. Even if we cannot change our mess, we can change how we view what to do about the mess. Dwelling without action leads to apathy. We can become so content sitting in our own filth that we never do anything to change it. Now, sometimes we might not always know what to do, but this is why God has given us His Word and people all around us to en-courage us and push us more toward the things of Him. This is why I am a counselor and why I believe in the power of Holy Spirit-guided therapy. We are not left to our own devices to know how to face the nasty things of this world. Thank God for His promises.

Sometimes, we need to just let stuff go. Carrying around hurt for years does nothing to the other person and everything to us. While these truths are all principles we know, it is much harder to make the choice to train our brains to live in freedom and peace. So many times, our society tells us that we need to play the victim card and that we can just live in the rut we find ourselves in. However, when Christ died on that cross, He did not intend for us to live beaten down for the rest of our lives.

There are moments when things in life happen that send us into a tailspin and often leave us perplexed. Struggle happens, and there are going to be seasons that do not feel awesome. But, through God's grace, we can overcome. Emotions are real, pain is real, but there is hope at the end of the tunnel. We have freedom in and through Christ.

Choose what you want to dwell on, and choose what you want to be your reality. Choose what you will let go of. Choose how you want to keep moving forward.

Discussion Questions

1. What do you need to let go of?

_____

_____

_____

_____

2. What do you choose to dwell on?

_____

_____

_____

_____

3. How has not letting go impacted your life?

_____

_____

_____

_____

Chapter 9
STRUGGLE ON

So, what do good little church girls look like? We look like normal people who struggle with normal things. However, we know the truth of who we are and anchor ourselves in the stable foundation that is Jesus Christ. We understand that Satan comes to steal, kill, and destroy, but that Jesus came to give us a full and vibrant life.[19] We know that we do not have to be defined by what we deal with, and we can live victorious lives no matter our struggle.

We do not have to live burdened by our past or by shame. We get the choice of who we want to be and how we want to shape our perspectives. Even when we feel like we have no control in our lives, we have the ability to control our minds. Our reactions, what we dwell on, and how we move forward are all up to us. We get to

---

[19] John 10:10

choose because God designed us that way. Contrary to popular belief, we do not have to live enslaved to our struggle, but we can find peace and rest in choosing to control our thoughts and keeping our eyes on the One who brings true peace and healing.

Don't ever fall into the trap of believing that you cannot change the rut you are stuck in. Scripture says that it is for freedom we were set free.[20] We were not set free to be bound by chains or to live shackled by an identity we were never meant to have. We were not set free to live burdened by the same struggles that have plagued us for the last decade, or to feel like we were never going to be able to escape the patterns we had established for ourselves. We were set free to walk in God-given victory.

My awareness of my own humanity has made me much more empathetic to others' humanity. When we live with our blinders on, we can become quite good at examining the sin we see in the lives of others while completely ignoring our own shortcomings. God opened my eyes to my own depravity, and that has made me that much more excited to help people find the victory that God has so graciously shown me. It does not mean that I live life free of struggle or do not have days when I need a good, holy smack. What it does mean is that I live a life not controlled by defeat but controlled by peace. It means I can keep my mind in check. I know that I get to shape the circumstances around me. This process is not something I have figured out how to execute perfectly, but that is okay. Life is about learning and growing, and, if we feel beaten down, we will not want to do either.

Life is a series of choices, and God has given us the tools to not

---

[20] Galatians 5:1

only make the right ones but to make ones that are ultimately for our good and His glory. Do not let who you were or the struggles that you face keep you from stepping into the purpose that God intends for you. When we are fixed on the past, on hurts, and on struggles, we can miss the divine direction that God has for our lives. Are you going to choose to serve your flesh or that nagging voice of shame telling you that you will never be effective in what God has asked you to do, or, are you going to follow the light that is beckoning you home into God's perfect will?

The moment I allowed myself to quit focusing so much on my struggles and actually got a handle on my thought life was the moment I was able to really see the beautiful purpose God had designed for me. If I had spent my life focused on the clutter, though I am still a work in progress on some days, I never would have heard God's voice telling me it was time to step into my God-given calling. I launched a ministry called Rebirth Ministries out of a desire to help others experience healing and wholeness, but I would not have heard God telling me to step out in faith into this new season of life if my focus were off. I would have missed out on the healing and wholeness God intended for me. I would not have been able to be used as God was desiring to use me.

My purpose has been clouded by temporal circumstances, struggle, and unnecessary, debilitating thoughts on more than one occasion. I have let the haunts of my past keep me from leaving them at Jesus' feet where they should be. We all allow struggles to have more power in our lives than we should, which keeps us from walking in the purpose and calling that God has for us. We need to heal, and then we need to throw our hurts and the things that kept us from being who God intended us to be into the metaphorical sea.

Once your struggle is dealt with, leave it dealt with and move forward into the victorious life God has for you. Once you know who you are, claim that identity and nothing else. Once you have told shame where it belongs, leave it at the cross. Once you have exposed the darkest parts of your heart, allow God's light to illuminate what only He can expose. Once you have found that army, trust that they are a beautiful gift from God meant to be an extension of His hands and His feet. Once you have let go of the notion that good little church girls don't face hardships and don't have human struggles, do not pick that notion back up again. Walk in the truth that your past does not define your present or your future and that no matter what you have faced, done, or gone through, God still desires to use you. He still chooses you.

The apostle Paul experienced a lot of struggle throughout his time on earth. He was shipwrecked, he was beaten, he was bitten by a viper, and ultimately, he was a martyr for the cause of Christ. But what words did he leave us? He said that he would BOAST in his weakness because it was in that weakness that Christ's strength was made perfect.[21] He understood that his purpose on this planet was not to have it all together all the time or to avoid persecution, but he understood that his purpose was in bringing glory to the name of God. Paul did not have an easy go of it, but we look to this man as a great man of the faith because he knew who he was, and he knew where his purpose was anchored. In the book of James, we are told to count it all joy when we face trials of any kind. Why is this? Because it produces perseverance, and when we let it have its full effect, it is made perfect in us that we might lack nothing.[22]

---

[21] 2 Corinthians 11:30
[22] James 1:2-4
82

When this world throws curveballs or when we have gotten ourselves into a bigger mess than we know what to do with, we must take our eyes off the circumstance and put them right back onto Jesus. Perspective changes everything. We cannot change circumstances, but we have the power to change how we frame those circumstances. We have the power to change where we allow our focus to be. When we look at our lives in light of the Gospel, we understand that nothing is too great for our great King. We understand that even though we face trials and temptations, we have already been given the victory. We understand that even though we are human and have pain, we have a place to lay that pain and to move forward.

Find that army who will walk with you, bathe yourself in the truth of God's Word, and remember that if God is for you, absolutely no one or nothing can be against you.[23] When you have a bad day, acknowledge it, learn from it, and move on. Do not keep holding onto the things of the past or what used to weigh you down. When you have made the choice to change your mind, do not let it go back to what it was. Live in your new way of thinking because this thinking is your victory. There is power in the name of Jesus to break every single chain in our lives, so let those chains fall off your life.

God wants us. Why does He want us? He wants us, despite our muck and mire, because we are wholly and dearly loved by our Heavenly Father. His grace, His unmerited favor and love washes over our hearts and renews us. Through God's grace, we are aware of our depravity, of our sin nature. We are also aware of just how much the cross means. Hear this today: God has chosen you; He has

---

[23] Romans 8:31

given you a place to belong and a home in the chaos of a sin-soaked world.

Through the process of figuring out whose and who I am, my fear of rejection is being replaced by my acceptance on the cross. My shame of struggling with homosexuality is replaced by the God-given identity I have—adoption into His royal family and a coheir with Christ. God wants to restore what was broken to make it something beautiful. He wants us to see the streams when it feels barren, and He wants us to know that we can and will overcome through the blood of Jesus Christ.

So, this is what good little church girls look like. They look like human beings who, in spite of struggle and hardship, understand who they are and where they are going. They understand that their struggles can either cripple them or help them see the restorative work of God in their lives. Choose today who you want to be and walk in that God-given freedom today and for the rest of the days to come.

Discussion Questions

1. How can you move forward in victory?

_____

_____

_____

_____

2. What do you want to be your truth?

_____

_____

_____

_____

3. What is the biggest lesson you have learned?

_____

_____

_____

_____

Made in the USA
Middletown, DE
12 March 2019